Table of Contents

You Might Be A Metalhead

by Don Jamieson & Joe Bartnick

Illustrated by Mike Morse
Cover Design by Vinnie Corbo
Produced and Edited by Vinnie Corbo

Published by Volossal Publishing
www.volossal.com

Copyright © 2016
ISBN 978-0-9968826-4-4

Dedication

To All The Bands I've Loved Before
- Don

To my ladies, Buns and the Boo.
- Joe

Introduction

This book is a humorous take on the world of hard rock and heavy metal by comedian and co-host Don Jamieson of *That Metal Show* and fellow comedian and metalhead, Joe Bartnick.

The title is a take off on Jeff Foxworthy's book *You Might Be A Redneck* but instead of blue collar comedy, it's more like black t-shirt comedy.

Heavy metal music has been so popular across six of the seven continents that it's literally an international language that is understood worldwide. And with Metallica playing Antarctica in December 2013 metal has finally conquered the entire world. It also explains the international popularity of *That Metal Show* now in it's 14th season. Metalheads everywhere will laugh their bullet belts off!

So, without any further ado, *You Might Be A Metalhead...*

You Might Be A Metalhead
Part One

If *Highway to Hell* was your wedding song.

If anytime you have chopstix, you drum.

If your dog doesn't have a chain but your wallet does.

If *Fight For Your Right To Party* is the
only rap song you like.

If you know how many moles Lemmy has on his face.

If you know Lemmy used to be a roadie for
Jimi Hendrix.

If you don't see the irony in the movie
Heavy Metal Parking Lot.

If you think bobbing your head is dancing.

If your biggest wet dream is seeing
Led Zeppelin with John Bonham.

If your favorite artist is the guy
who does the Iron Maiden album covers.

If Ted Nugent is the only Republican you think is cool.

If when you were 12, you would rather read
Circus or *Hit Parader* than *Playboy*.

If you look through a band's CD's at a store
even though you own them all.

If your hair gets caught under your pillow
when you sleep.

If Yoo Hoo is the most nutritious thing you drink.

If your life philosophy is
"There are two paths you can go by..."

If your leather jacket is the warmest coat you own.

If at some point in the mid-80's, you had a mullet.
Or still do.

If you dress your kid as Slash for Halloween.

If your car is older than your girlfriend.

Metal Six Packs
Part One

Because nothing goes better with metal than a 6-pack!

Top 6 Songs To Get A Lap Dance To

1) *Girls, Girls, Girls* - Mötley Crüe

When Mötley Crüe announced their farewell tour in 2014 every 50 year-old stripper in America shed a tear. But even if it takes until they're 80 to strip their way through college, this has and will always be the National Anthem of Go-Go Dancers. The list of clubs mentioned in the song is on every degenerate metal head's bucket list.

2) *You Shook Me All Night Long* - AC/DC

A very close second to Mötley. Kind of like having Joe DiMaggio and Mickey Mantle in the same lineup. With all the money we've spent on lap dances over the years this song should be known as *You Shook Me DOWN All Night Long.*

3) *Pour Some Sugar On Me* - Def Leppard

Phil Collen of Def Leppard actually said on *That Metal Show* that the reason this song became big is because strippers in Florida started dancing to it. You want a hit? Don't give it to some promotion or marketing executive. Give it to every Go-Go Dancer in Ft. Lauderdale! Sugar is great sweetener but when we're at a strip club all we wanna see is the pink stuff.

4) *Crazy Bitch* - **Buckcherry**

"Crazy" and "Bitch" are positive affirmations in the stripper world and we're all about positivity. Crazy and strippers go hand in hand like Rockin' and Dokken. Also makes a decent quinceañera song.

5) *Cherry Pie* - **Warrant**

Ok the lyrics don't exactly bring to mind John Lennon's *Imagine* but when you have a juicy, round ass bouncing in your face the only thing you're trying to imagine is eating her cherry pie.

6) *Closer* - **Nine Inch Nails**

Yeah, she'll "f*ck you like an animal" ...out of 200 bucks. This song oozes pure sex. Imagine a young, fully-stacked dancer grinding and writhing on you while *Closer* plays in the background. Then, imagine going into the bathroom afterwards and cleaning out your underwear. Just us?

Honorable Mention: *Living Dead Girl* - **Rob Zombie**

Because pale-white, goth strippers with cadaver makeup that smell of patchouli need something to dance to.

Top 6 Songs About Heavy Duty Hunnies

1) *Whole Lotta Rosie* - **AC/DC**

You know what they say...write about what you know. When a band uses a 90-foot tall inflatable fat chick as a stage prop for a song, you know they've had a few tubbies in their day. Plus 42-39-56 always made a great high school locker combination and we've never met a skinny Rosie.

2) *Fat Bottomed Girls* - **Queen**

An absolute anthem dedicated to all the ladies with gargantuan glutes. Teenagers nowadays have unlimited nudity and deviant sex acts just a mouse-click away. When we were young, the poster that came with the *Jazz* album with all the naked chicks on bikes was OUR porn. *Fat Bottomed Girls* did make the world go 'round because unlike Perfect Bottomed Girls, they put out to metal heads.

3) *Unskinny Bop* - **Poison**

Even in his heyday of getting A-list trim, Bret Michaels would probably throw a fattie a bone and bone one once in a while. If you eat at Jean Georges every night, eventually you're gonna have a craving for Waffle House.

4) *Thunder Thighs* - **Ted Nugent**

Uncle Ted, who has written some of the greatest love songs of all time like *Wango Tango, Yank Me, Crank Me* and *Wang Dang Sweet Poontang* adds this little ditty dedicated to big-legged women who do have soul. Otherwise know as Ted's 'Big Bang Theory'.

5) *Spit* - **KISS**

When it comes to groupies, Gene Simmons has never been one to discriminate. Most of the chicks in his Polaroids needed a wide-angle lens. We still can't believe he hasn't marketed a KISS fat femme blow up doll. They could call her *Christine Sixteen Hundred Pounds*.

6) *Spandex Enormity* - **MOD**

We've never understood why heavy duty hunnies always wear spandex? It's like they're trying to confuse you into thinking they're smaller until they take them off and RELEASE THE KRAKEN. It's kind of like a guy with a small penis buying Magnum condoms in hopes that he'll one day fit into them. Not that we'd know or anything.

Honorable Mention: *Big Bottom* - **Spinal Tap**

Top 6 Bands That Sound Like Dark Ages Diseases

1) Megadeth

2) Deep Purple

3) Krokus

4) Amorphis

5) Gorgoroth

6) Hirax

Honorable Mentions: Triptykon, Amon Amarth, Montrose, Helix, Slough Feg, Watain, GWAR.

If one of these doesn't kill ya, the Celtic Frost certainly will!

Top 6 Favorite Metal Funnies

1) Beavis and Butthead

This animated juggernaut was not only stupidly funny, it helped skyrocket the careers of many hard rock and metal bands, none more than Rob Zombie. Winger, not so much.

2) Sam Kinison

When Sam did his *Wild Thing* video he got everyone from Slash to Jon Bon Jovi to Tommy Lee to show up for the out-of-control party extravaganza. He also fell asleep inside of Jessica Hahn. What's more metal than that???

3) Spinal Tap

Some claim it was inspired by Saxon. Others say UFO. Years later Black Sabbath pulled an opposite-Spinal Tap when they had Stonehenge pieces made for one of their tours and they were too BIG to fit into any of the venues they were playing. There's truly a fine line between reality and absurdity.

4) Andrew Dice Clay

Wrote rhymes that were dirtier and funnier than Bon Scott and proudly wore leather like Rob Halford. You know, without the trips to the men's bathhouse.

5) Metalocalypse

Themes of violence, death, the macabre and hyperbolic black humor. No, not Hello Kitty. It's Metalocalypse on Adult Swim, a cartoon that features a fictitious death metal band called Dethklok. Which then became a real death metal band. Which is a helluva lot better than a real Hello Kitty band.

6) Metallica: Some Kind Of Monster

Metallica in therapy? Dave Mustaine crying? *LuLu*? Now THAT'S comedy!

Top 6 Tunes To Eat Your Neighbor To

There are times when you're just sitting at home wondering what to crank up on the old stereo. You're looking California but feeling Jeffrey Dahmer so you reach for your Cannibal mix tape and pop it in. What's that you say? You don't have one? Well you should. And here are the 6 deviant delights that should be on it. Also, it's funny that you still have a tape player.

1) *Butchered at Birth* - **Cannibal Corpse**

With a name like Cannibal Corpse you're a ringer for this category. From the album of the same name, this grotesque golden oldie shreds at the frantic pace of a murder in progress. You can almost picture the oozing bile, bladder spurting urine and zombie masturbation. You know, if you're already a serial killer.

2) *Pleasures of the Flesh* - **Exodus**

From the excellent *Bonded By Blood* album this murderous melody starts with the beat of primitive drums warning you that you are about to enter unwelcome territory. But alas, it's too late! You stumble upon a tribe of hungry cannibals in the jungle who are on the hunt for dinner. And guess who just became the main course?

33

3) *She-Wolf* - Megadeth

From *Cryptic Writings* this terrifying tune tells of a wicked temptress with mystic lips and lusting eyes. Out of all the ways to die this seems like the sexiest. Who wants to be disemboweled in Ed Gein's farmhouse when you can be devoured by the sexy She-Wolf?

4) *Headhunter* - Krokus

The title track off their classic 1983 album. Let's face it, nothing goes better with sex, drugs, rock n' roll than a big, heaping serving of human flesh. Whenever we listen to this homicidal hymn we have nightmares of being chased with an axe by a flesh-crazed Fernando Von Arb.

5) *Mein Teil* - Rammstein

Off their fourth album *Reise, Reise* which we're guessing means *Rise, Rise* in German. This Deutsche ditty is based on the true story of two men who meet & one agrees to be eaten by the other. Including the penis. It's one thing to be a cannibal. But a gay, German cannibal...c'mon?

6) *Live Undead* - Slayer

Slayer loves documenting atrocities to the dead. Disguises crafted from rotting flesh in *Dead Skin Mask*, sex with a cadaver in *Necrophiliac* and now *they're* eaten in this graveyard classic from *South Of Heaven*. If we had to have our bodies desecrated and/or defiled by any band it would be by Slayer's hand. They seem to know what they're doing.

Honorable Mentions:

Predator - Carnivore
Eating The Cannibals - Heaven & Hell
Eat The Rich - Mötorhead

Pair any of these with a blood-red glass of wine and cap off with a chapter or two from the cannibalistic classic *Alive*.

You Might Be A Metalhead
Part Two

If the Kiss Army is the only army you'd join.

If no one liked you in high school.

If carrying your amp is your only workout.

If you think posters are art.

If you think Sammy Hagar ruined Van Halen.

If you still air drum that part in *Tom Sawyer* by Rush even though you've heard that song a million times.

If the only song you dance to at weddings is *You Shook Me All Night Long*.

If you carry a zippo that doesn't have fluid in it.

If you give your woman all your contraband
to bring into the concert.

If your Mom is your designated driver.

If all of your favorite music is on cassette.

If you always have a guitar pick in your pocket.

If Road Warriors are you favorite wrestlers because they came out to *Iron Man*.

If you know the spoken word piece at the beginning of *Number Of The Beast* word for word.

If you hear the name Great White and think of the band instead of the man-eating species of shark.

If you know that the bass line from Megadeth's *Peace Sells But Who's Buying* was once the MTV News theme.

If it takes you three tries to go through the TSA.

If your idea of "scrapbooking" is saving
all your concert stubs.

If you pray to Rob Halford, the Metal God.

If you mail-ordered Metallica's *Kill Em All*.

If 'Sabbath' to you is a band with Geezer on bass
and not a 'day of rest.'

If you blast AC/DC's *Sin City* as you cruise
down THE STRIP.

If to you Iron Maiden is a band,
not a medieval torture device.

If every time you're with the old gang
you think of Thin Lizzy.

If the *only* police you like is *The Dream Police*.

Metal Six Packs
Part Twö

6 Ways To Know The Opener Sucks

1) They thank the headliner after every song.

2) They drop the 'F' bomb constantly.

3) They play on 11.

4) They play an encore.

5) They say they wish had more time.

6) They sit on stools while they play.

6 Things Metal Bands Do
That Other Bands Don't

1) They bring every guitar they have to a show.

2) They use a full Marshall stack to play a local bar.

3) They not only have a band name, they have their own logo and font.

4) They put 'drum solo' in their set list.

5) They wear t-shirts of more successful bands.

6) They don't consider the keyboard player essential.

Top 6 Heavy Metal Movies

1) *Maximum Overdrive*
AC/DC, talking trucks and Emilio Estevez.

2) *The Song Remains The Same*
It used to be all we had.

3) *KISS Meets The Phantom of The Park*
Who's scarier, the Phantom or Gene?

4) *Dead Pool*
Dirty Harry and Axl Rose.

5) *Strangeland*
Dee Snider brings Captain Howdy comes to life.

6) *Heavy Metal*
Duh.

Top 6 Songs Played at a Hockey Game

1) *Welcome To The Jungle* - Guns N' Roses
Hopefully this jock jam inspires athletes to give their all and not to show up 2 hours late for the game.

2) *Rock You Like A Hurricane* - Scorpions
An undeniable hard rock anthem and the equivalent of heavy metal steroids.

3) *Thunderstruck* - AC/DC
This Aussie Anthem will get you more jacked up than an over-caffeinated Zakk Wylde at the local Gold's Gym.

4) *Enter Sandman* - Metallica
This Metalli-classic will get the home team and crowd more pumped up than A-Rod after a Biogenesis delivery.

5) *Running With The Devil* - Van Halen
    More epic than Eddie Van Halen's feathered hair and Dave's high leg kicks.

6) *Crazy Train* - Ozzy Osbourne
    This crazy classic could get any team pumped up to play. Or at least bite the head off a dove or wiz on the Alamo.

Editors note: We actually could have used all AC/DC songs.

Top 6 Albums Metal Heads Use As An Aphrodisiac

1) *Slippery When Wet* - **Bon Jovi**

Between Jon and Richie dueting on *Wanted Dead or Alive* and power ballads like *I'd Die For You* even Screech from *Saved By The Bell* could lay some pipe to this album. Bon Jovi helped more dudes get laid than cheap beer.

2) *Hysteria* - **Def Leppard**

Pyromania might be the first album you ever finger-banged a girl to but *Hysteria* is the one that made you *Armageddon It*.

3) *The Great Radio Controversy* - **Tesla**

If you timed it right and got her naked by the time *Love Song* came on, you were definitely gonna rock the arena between her legs.

4) *Open Up And Say...Ahh* - **Poison**

Play that album in the throes of passion and hope she takes a hint from the title.

5) *Lita* - **Lita Ford**

This was a great one because it had the ballad *Close My Eyes Forever* so you at least got some Ozzy in the mix. Plus if you closed your eyes, you got the added bonus of pretending you were banging Lita. You weren't.

6) *Skid Row* - **Skid Row**

The best way to get into an 18 year-old chick's pants was to listen to a band whose singer LOOKED LIKE an 18 year-old chick.

You Might Be A Metalhead
Part Three

If you wore a British flag t-shirt because Joe Elliot from Def Leppard wore one in the *Photograph* video.

If you bought all 4 Kiss solo albums and linked
the puzzle pieces together on your wall.

If 99% of your wardrobe is black.

If you know where the umlauts go on
Motorhead and Motley Crue. (think quick!)

If you never watch any band below
the second band on bill.

If you tailgate before show to save money.

If your only workout equipment
are forearm squeezers.

If you have spent days with *Powerage* as the
only thing you've listened too.

If you puke in the parking lot before the show
but still go in. And still drink.

If you go swimming in cut-off jean shorts.

If the *Turbo* album made you vomit.

If you associate an Axl, Clutch and Crowbar
with music instead of a car.

If it's not the Union Jack,
its Def Leppard's underwear.

If you have no idea what the Italian "Maloik" is
but you do know what the "Devil Horns" are.

If you have *Night Flights* on VHS.

If you don't know the name of your school mascot but
you know Iron Maiden's mascot's name is Eddie.

If you use a lighter, not cell phone, during the ballad.

If you think dressing up is wearing
your best concert shirt.

If your wristbands are leather.

If you have actually "Stumped The Trunk."

If you write a book called *You Might Be A Metalhead*.

If this is the longest book
you've ever read.

About The Authors

Don Jamieson is currently co-hosting VH1 Classic's hit heavy metal talk show series, *That Metal Show* where legends of rock hang out to discuss their past and current projects in front of a live studio audience full of metal maniacs.

Rolling Stone Magazine dubbed *That Metal Show* one of the 50 Best Reasons To Watch TV! He is also a co-host on *Beer Money*, a fast-paced, non-traditional sports quiz show airing on SNY (SportsNet New York).

Amongst his many accomplishments, Jamieson's 1st stand-up CD *Live & Hilarious* on Metal Blade Records hit the Top 20 on iTunes comedy charts & his brand new one *Hell Bent For Laughter* peaked at #9. He also performed stand-up at Metallica's Orion Music + More Festival and was introduced by drummer Lars Ulrich. He is proudly sponsored by Monster Energy Drinks & Coldcock Whiskey.

Jamieson's proudest moment is becoming an "Emmy Award-Winner" for his work on HBO's "Inside The NFL." Don and long-time comedy partner, Jim Florentine, lent their brand of humor to the popular sports show; writing, producing and performing sports-themed comedy sketches.

Don started his career as one of the young and talented comedy minds at MTV helping to launch the careers of comics like Jon Stewart, Kevin James and Tom Green. But unbeknownst to many, Don was spending his nights on the local comedy scene developing his own comic style. He is currently in production for the FOURTEENTH season of *That Metal Show* and his SECOND season of *Beer Money*.

Joe Bartnick was born and raised in Pittsburgh, PA where he learned to eat, drink and be funny. He moved to San Francisco and began his career as a standup comic working his way up from performing in coffee shops and laundry mats to play prestigious venues such as *The Warfield* and becoming a regular at the world famous *Punchline*.

Joe moved to Los Angeles and jumped into writing and acting. In LA, Joe has written on many television projects including the *ESPYS*, *The NFL on FOX*, *Snoop After Dark* and Eddie Griffin's *Going for Broke*. As an actor Joe starred in *Dirty Jokes the Movie*. Joe created and starred (fully clothed) in the Playboy TV series *King of Clubs*.

Joe performed a closing set on AXS-TV's *Live at Gotham*. For many years Joe wrote and opened for the Queen of Mean, Lisa Lampanelli. He can now be seen opening for Bill Burr or headlining on his own or as part of the *All In Tour* with Paul Virzi.

One of Joe's biggest thrills was roasting Motley Crue's Tommy Lee on Tommy Lee's show *Battleground Earth*. Joe also wrote the best selling e-book *You Might Be a Douchebag* which is now bigger and better and out in paperback.

Joe has parlayed his love of hockey into the highly successful podcast *Puck Off* and contributes a comedy column to *Pro Hockey News*. In 2014, Joe went back to his roots by talking hockey on a segment called *Soft Dumps* on Pittsburgh's legendary rock station WDVE.

Joe's CD *Salute!* can be purchased from iTunes, Amazon, CD Baby and other fine audio locations.

Just for the record, Joe HATES the band RUSH and thinks Cinderella is criminally underrated.

Other Books From Volossal Publishing

You Might Be A Douchebag
Is Your Boyfriend Really Your Girlfriend?
Fetish and You
Sex, Fetish and Him
A Boy In Hiding
Tamales For Gringos
Cartoons That Will Send Me Straight To Hell
The Astrology Sex Diet
Jesus, Hitler, Manson and Me
The El
You've Got The Balls, Use Them!
Confessions of a Fat Player
Feeding The Beast
Why Not If It Works
Online Dating Advice
The Lunch
Different Drummer

Volossal Publishing
www.volossal.com

You Might Be A Metalhead

CPSIA information can be obtained
at www.ICGtesting.com
Printed in the USA
FFOW05n1843120416